W[illegible]ere no di[illegible]oday?

FOX EYE
PUBLISHING

Why are there no dinosaurs alive today?

Most people think they all died because the world suddenly changed.

Why did the world suddenly change?

Because a huge rock
from space hit the earth.

Why did that change the world?

When the rock hit the ground it caused earthquakes ...

... volcanic eruptions, and giant waves everywhere.

Nearly everything was broken, burned, or flooded.

So why are there animals alive now?

Not everything died.
Some of the smaller
animals survived.

So, maybe there could be smaller dinosaurs alive today?

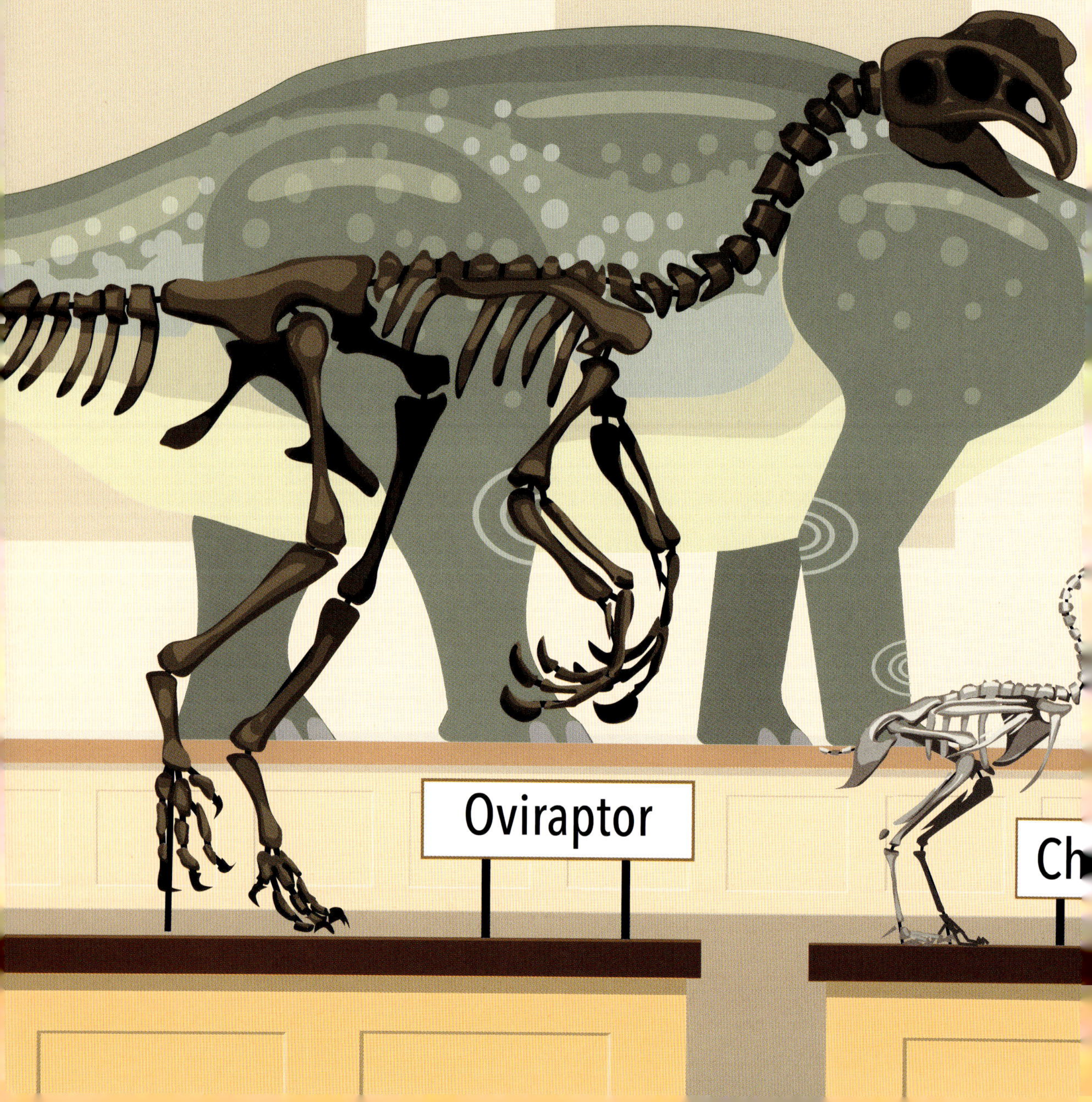

Perhaps there are. Some scientists think that over time they may have changed into birds.

What do you think?

Let's find out about Dinosaurs

Turn the page over to discover the answers to these questions.

When did the dinosaurs live?

What was the largest dinosaur?

How do we know about Dinosaurs?

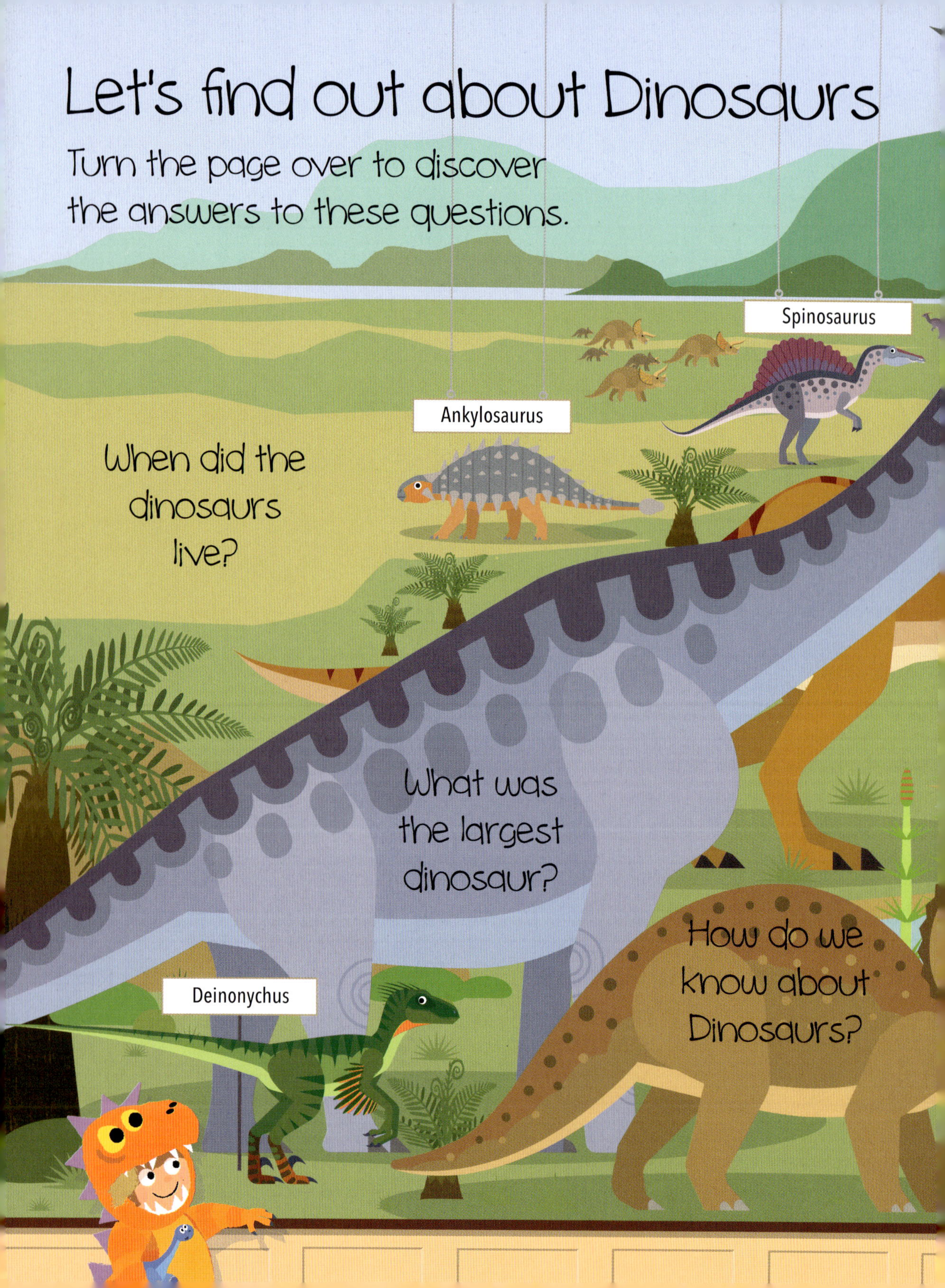

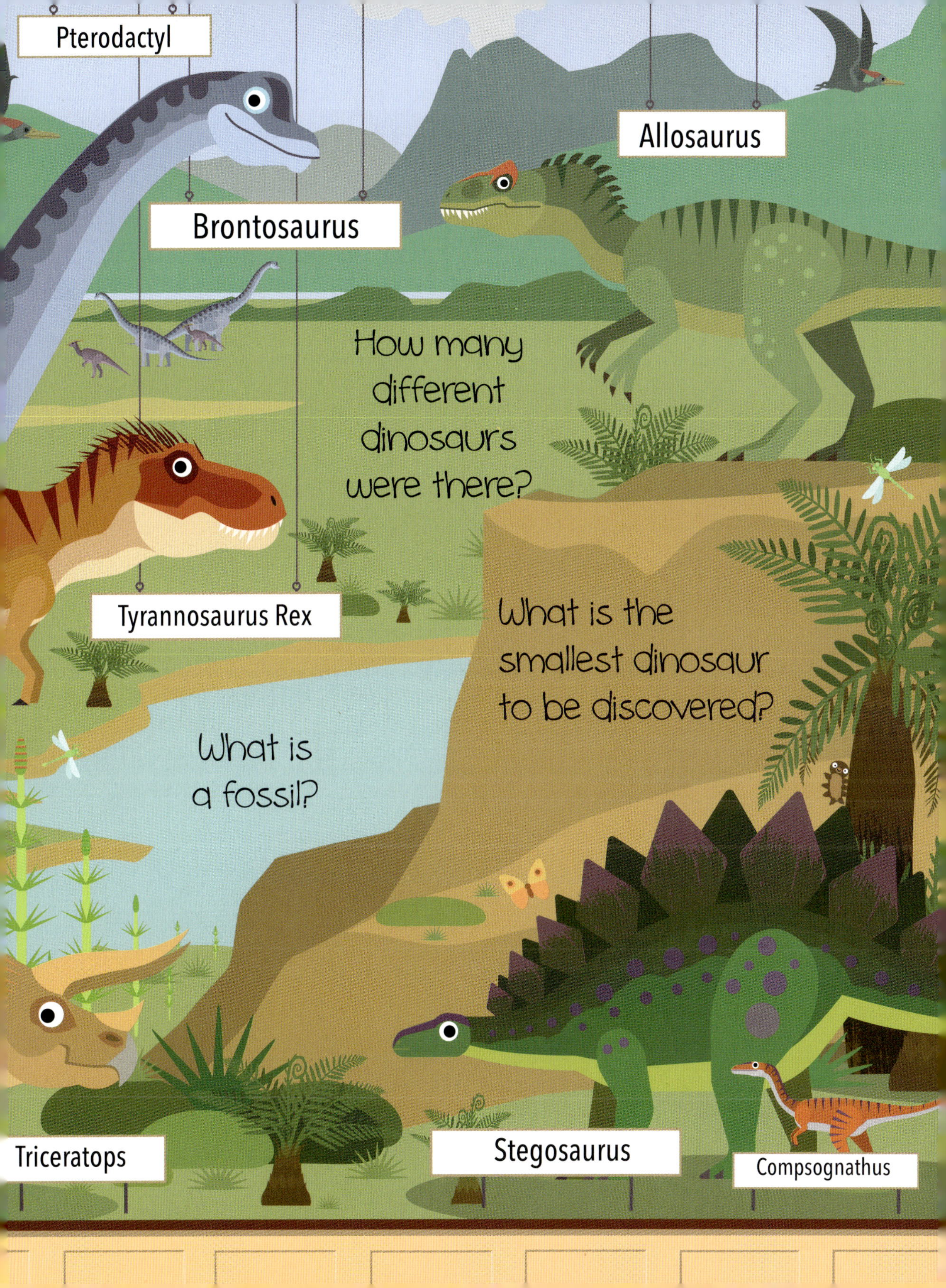
Pterodactyl
Allosaurus
Brontosaurus
How many different dinosaurs were there?
Tyrannosaurus Rex
What is the smallest dinosaur to be discovered?
What is a fossil?
Triceratops
Stegosaurus
Compsognathus

Let's find out about Dinosaurs

The answers are...

About
235–66 million
years ago.

Argentinosaurus
huinculensis.
It weighed up to 96.4
metric tons.

By studying their
fossilised bones,
eggs, and footprints.

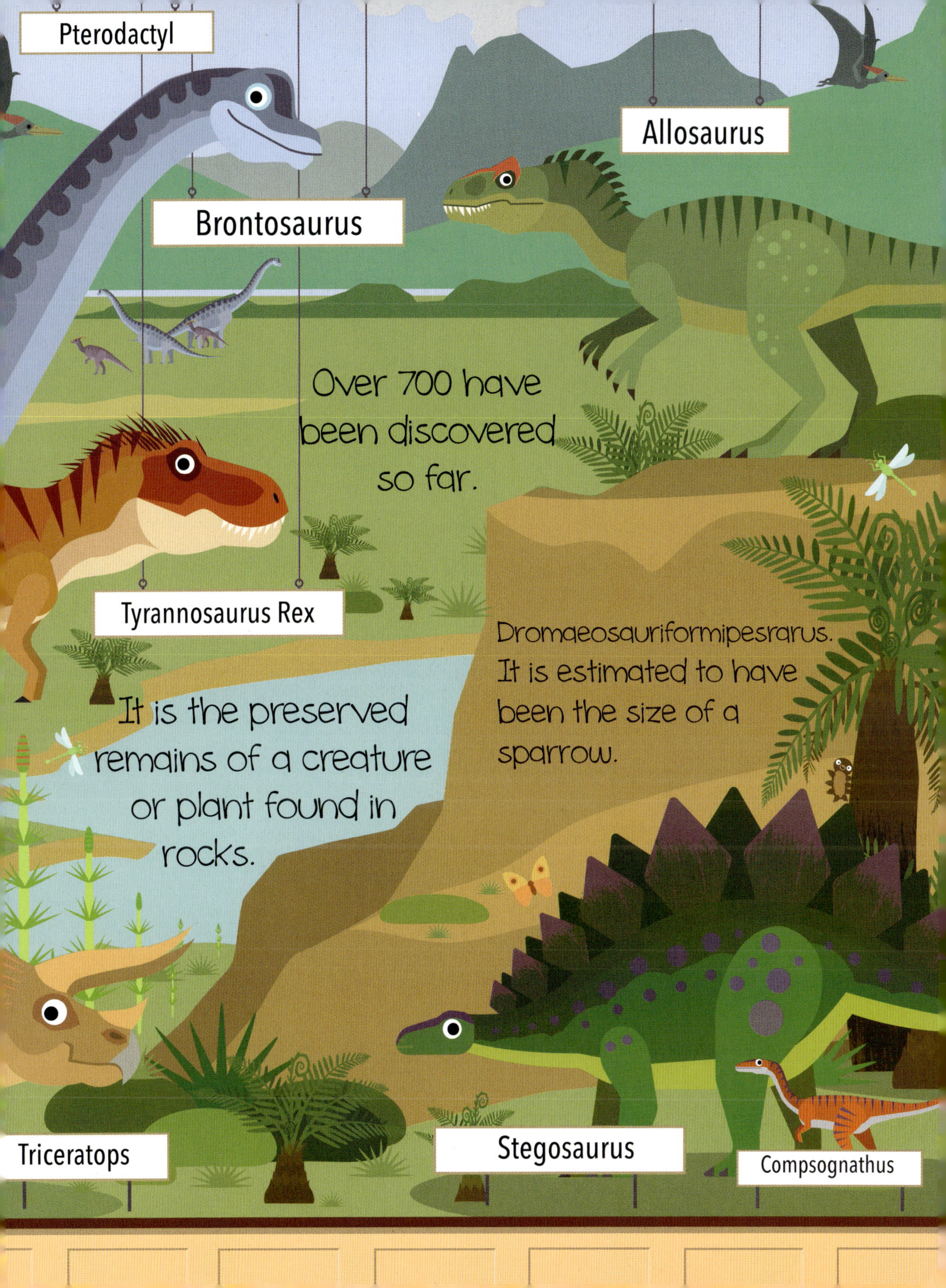
Pterodactyl
Allosaurus
Brontosaurus
Over 700 have been discovered so far.
Tyrannosaurus Rex
Dromaeosauriformipesrarus. It is estimated to have been the size of a sparrow.
It is the preserved remains of a creature or plant found in rocks.
Triceratops
Stegosaurus
Compsognathus

How to use this book

You can read this book with one child or a group of children.

The book can be used to begin a discussion around complex questions such as learning why there are no dinosaurs today.

The book is also a reading aid, with enlarged and repeated words to help children to develop their reading skills.

How to read the story

Before beginning the story, ensure that the children you are reading to are relaxed and focused.

Take time to look at the enlarged words and the illustrations, and discuss what this book might be about before reading the story.

New words can be tricky for young children to approach.

Sounding them out first, slowly and repeatedly, can help children to learn the words and become familiar with them.

Did you spot
the Tardigrade
hiding in
this book?

First published in 2023 by Fox Eye Publishing
Unit 31, Vulcan House Business Centre,
Vulcan Road, Leicester, LE5 3EF
www.foxeyepublishing.com

Written and illustrated by Simon Couchman

ISBN 978-1-80445-351-3

A catalogue record for this book is available from the British Library.

Printed in China

Titles in the Series

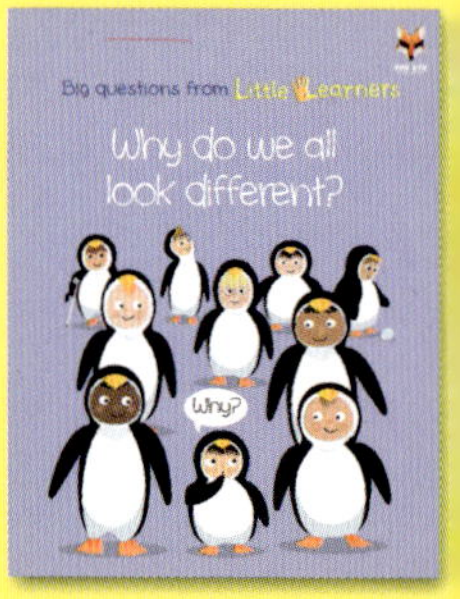

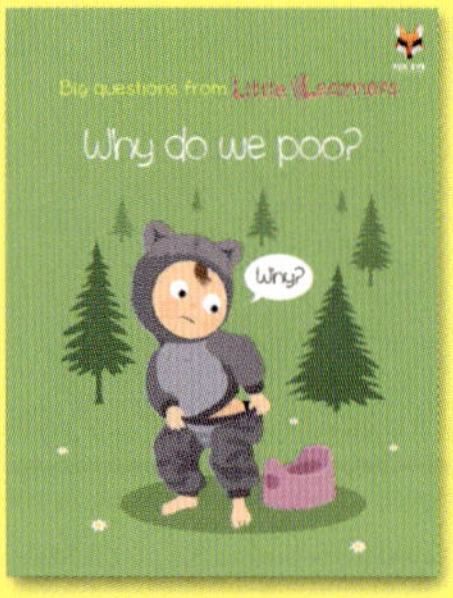

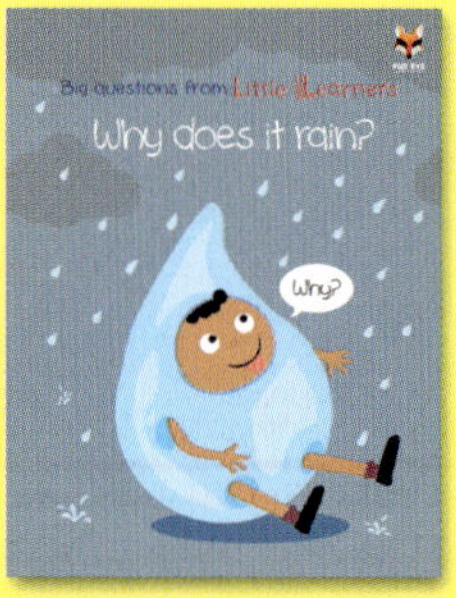